I'm Reading About

KANSAS

The Sunflower State!

GALLOPADE

by Carole Marsh

Printed and Manufactured in Peachtree City, GA., USA
www.gallopade.com

Book design: John Hanson

Editorial manager: Janice Baker

Kansas is a great state.

It is one of a kind.

What makes Kansas special?

Let's read about it

and see!

NATIVE AMERICANS

Who lived in Kansas first?

Native Americans did!

They moved around to find food.
They hunted animals for food to eat.
They fished in Kansas' rivers.
They gathered fruits and seeds and nuts.

EXPLORERS

The first explorers came to Kansas in 1541.
They came from the country of Spain.

Francisco Vásquez de Coronado was their leader.
He and his men were looking for gold and new land!

EPM

SETTLEMENT

Many Americans traveled west through Kansas in the mid 1800s. Some of them decided to settle in Kansas. One of the first settlements was Fort Leavenworth. The town of Leavenworth was built near the fort.

Leavenworth is located along the Missouri River.

Leavenworth

STATEHOOD

Kansas was the 34th state
to join the United States of America!

Isn't it great,
to be a state!
I bet Kansas
could hardly wait!

Kansas became a state in 1861.

Kansas

The 34th State

FLAG

I am the state flag.

What color am I?
I am blue.

Look at me.
What else do you see?

I fly high over the state of Kansas!

AD ASTRA PER ASPERA
KANSAS

CAPITAL

Say hello to Topeka,
the capital city of Kansas!

There is an important building in Topeka.
It is the State Capitol.
Kansas laws are made there!

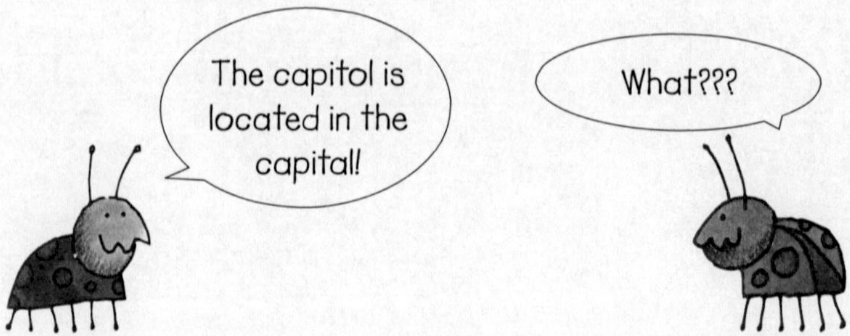

Capitol
Topeka
Capital

SEAL

I am a seal,
but I am not the State Seal.
If I were, I would be very important.
I would be stamped on many official papers.
(Ouch, that might hurt!)

GREAT SEAL OF THE STATE OF KANSAS
AD ASTRA PER ASPERA
JANUARY 29, 1861

Now, that's official!

NICKNAME

State nicknames are fun!
State nicknames are great!
They share fun facts
about each state!

Kansas's nickname is "The Sunflower State."

Bright yellow sunflowers grow all over Kansas!

The Sunflower State

BORDERS

Look at Kansas.
Kansas is in a region called "the Midwest."

Kansas borders four other states.
Find them on the map!

Borders

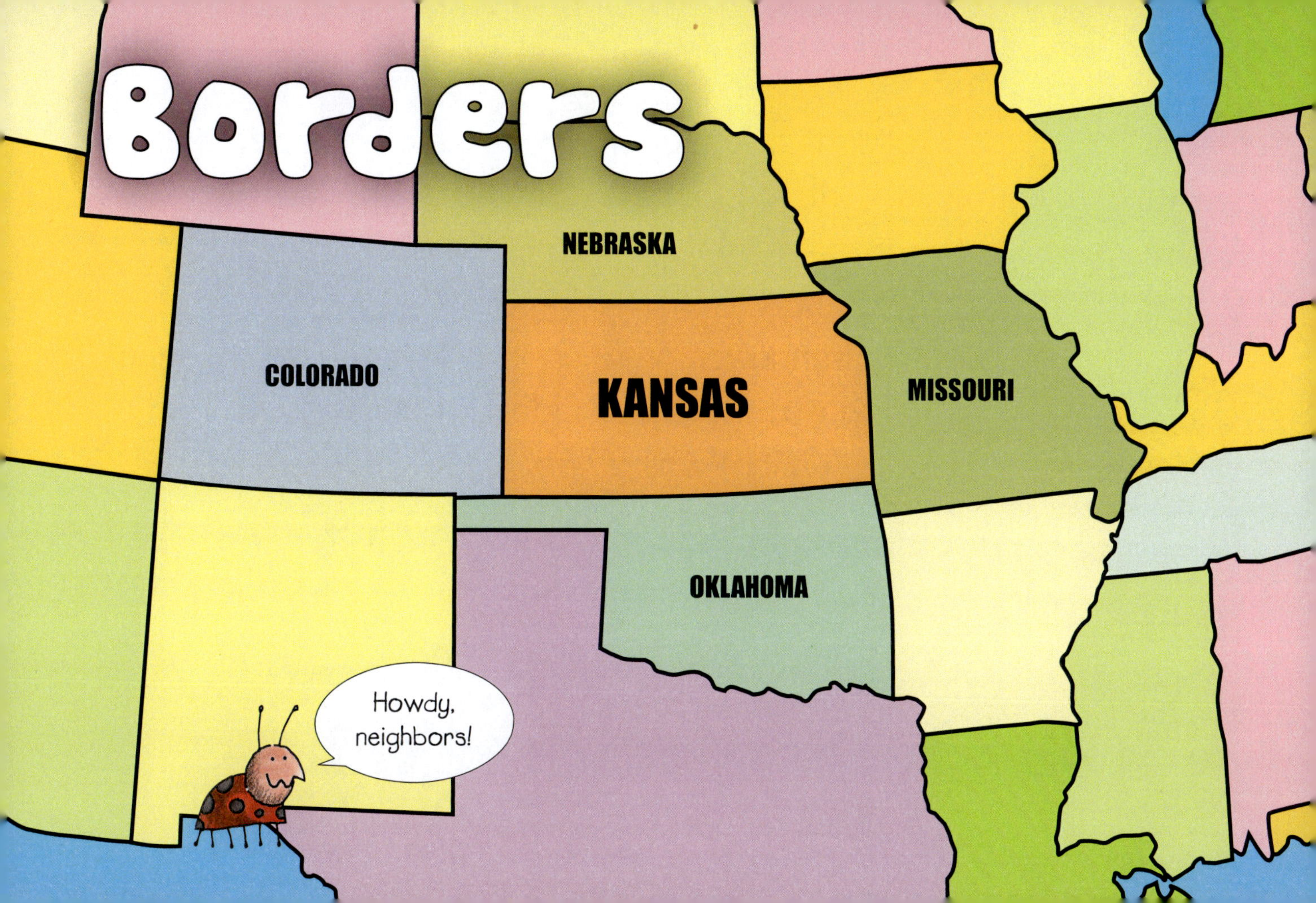
NEBRASKA
COLORADO
KANSAS
MISSOURI
OKLAHOMA
Howdy, neighbors!

PRESIDENT

Dwight Eisenhower was the 34th President of the United States of America. He grew up in Kansas!

Dwight Eisenhower grew up in a town called Abilene. He was the third-oldest of seven boys! Dwight was a very good athlete. Football was his favorite sport.

Dwight Eisenhower

PEOPLE

Many famous people

James Naismith

Invented the game of basketball using a peach basket

Walter Chrysler

Founded the automobile maker Chrysler

Russell Stover

Chemist who founded Russell Stover candies

Call our state home!

PEOPLE

Amelia Earhart

First woman pilot to fly solo across the Atlantic Ocean

Gwendolyn Brooks

Poet who became the first African American to win a Pulitzer Prize

Robert Dole

World War II hero and U.S. Senator from Kansas

Western Meadowlark

BIRD

I am the state bird, and I fly
over Kansas, proud and high.

As I fly, up in the sky,
I flap my wings to tell you "Hi!"

The Kansas state bird is the Western Meadowlark.

Wild Native Sunflower

I am the Wild Native Sunflower.
I am the state flower.

I grow where it's warm and sunny.
I bloom in summer and fall.
I help make Kansas beautiful!

Look at me! Smell me!
I grow on tall stalks!

Cottonwood Tree

TREE

I am a Cottonwood tree—I'm the state tree.
All over Kansas is where to find me.

My roots run deep, they keep me strong.
I can live more than 70 years—that's very long!

I stand up straight, big and tall.
Don't climb too high—it would hurt to fall!

Honeybee

INSECT

I am the Honeybee.
I am the state insect.

I might sting you if you bother me.
But really, I am your friend.

I carry pollen from flower to flower.
I make honey.
I help Kansas crops grow.

BZZZZZZZZZZZ!

Great Plains

GREAT PLAINS

Kansas lies within the Great Plains.
The tall golden grass
sways in the breeze.

The Great Plains has rolling hills,
and not many trees.
It stretches as far as the eye can see!

The Great Plains are home to many animals:

Prairie Dogs **Red Foxes** **Hawks** **Gophers** **and More!**

Lakes

LAKES

Let's go to the lake!

We can wade in the water.
We can ride on a boat.

We can jump off the dock
onto an inner tube float!

The largest lake in Kansas is Milford Lake.

Rivers

RIVERS

Kansas has many rivers.
People like to use rivers for boating and fishing!

This habitat is home to many animals:

Birds Deer Snakes Frogs Fish and More!

Topeka is located along the Kansas River.

Strataca

LANDMARK

There is a place in Kansas called Strataca.
Strataca is an underground salt mine.
Visitors can go 650 feet underground.
The salt mine has walls and floors made of salt!

Strataca used to be an active salt mine.
Miners removed the salt
and left large salt caves.

Kansas Crops

Kansas has many farms.
Why?
Because Kansas has good soil and a mild climate!

Some of the top crops grown in Kansas are:

Wheat **Sorghum** **Corn** **Soybeans**

Sports in Kansas

Baseball! Basketball! Football! Soccer!
Kansas has it all.

Whether you like to watch or play,
You are sure to have a ball!

Sporting Kansas City

Wildcats

Jayhawks

Shockers

& More!

Kansas: The Breadbasket of the World

CLAIM TO FAME

Kansas is known as the Breadbasket of the World. Kansas grows more wheat than any other U.S. state! Wheat is used to make bread, cereal, pasta, and many more products.

Did you know wheat is used to make paper, adhesive on postal stamps, and charcoal?

GLOSSARY

adhesive: glue

climate: weather conditions in an area over a long period of time

elect: to choose someone by voting

habitat: a place where plants or animals naturally live

laws: rules made by the government

pollen: a yellow powder that helps plants make new plants

region: an area that has similar characteristics

settlement: the first community in an area

solo: something done by one person

sorghum: a grain often used for animal feed